COPYWRITING

10 TIPS TO WRITE
THE PERFECT AD

FAUSTINO GÓMEZ VALERO

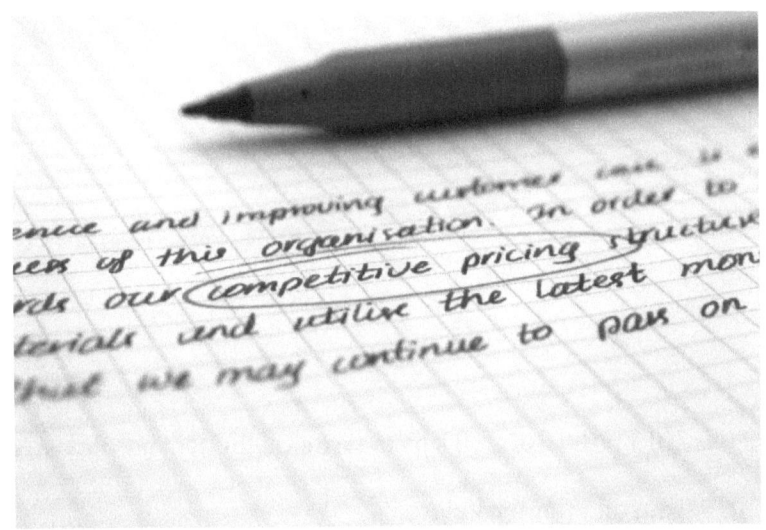

Title: COPYWRITING - 10 tips to write the perfect ad

2019, Faustino Gómez Valero

1st edition

kind, express or implied. Readers acknowledge that the author is not involved in the provision of legal, financial, medical or professional advice.

By reading this document, the reader agrees that under no circumstances are we liable for any losses, direct or indirect, incurred as a result of the use of the information contained in this document, including, but not limited to, errors, omissions or inaccuracies.

TABLE OF CONTENTS

WHY DID I WRITE THIS BOOK?

As an entrepreneur and digital business consultant for many years I have seen hundreds of companies and freelancers invest large amounts of time and money in launching online businesses, which they are then unable to make profitable due to their lack of selling capacity.

It is useless if you manage to set up the best online store, with the best products at the best prices, if then you are not able to get buyers to your website.

There are those who believe that by investing large amounts of money in ad campaigns such as Google Ads or Facebook Ads, the results are guaranteed, but this is not the case. A huge advertising campaign without the right ad texts is like throwing banknotes into the fire, as your campaigns will only serve to squander your money.

With the right ads, I have seen how advertising campaigns of only a couple of euros a day, with bids of only a few cents per click, have managed to give their creators spectacular results.

Remember that in marketing, as in other areas of life, quality matters more than quantity.

Find out what points will make your ads stand out from the rest of the market!

WHY SHOULD YOU READ THIS BOOK?

This book will make you change your point of view on the world of marketing in general, and digital marketing in particular.

Today you can find thousands of editors on the net willing to write the texts of your ads and advertising campaigns, but how do you know you're not throwing money away?

With this book you will discover what your potential customers are looking for, what they want to see and how you can awaken in them the need to purchase your products or services.

Sales is an art, and here we'll show you the ten commandments of commercial art.

You have two options to master the art of sales. The first is to continue creating meaningless advertising campaigns, with which it is impossible to achieve returns, and learn from your own mistakes. This option, without a doubt, is the slowest and the one that will cost you the most money.

The second option is to buy this book for a few dollars and start applying our advice so that your advertising campaigns finally start giving the results they deserve, or not.

What is advertising?

Is it something to be considered as a work of beauty or art? Are they intelligent slogans or funny prose? Is labor to be judged by an award or recognition?

It's nothing like that.

Advertising is the **sales capacity multiplied**.

That's all.

And the purpose of advertising, or copywriting, is the **printed sale**.

The purpose of a copywriter's job is to sell. That's it.

Selling is achieved by persuasion with the written word, much like a television commercial that sells (if done correctly) by persuading with images and audio.

As Claude Hopkins wrote in his timeless classic, *Scientific Advertising*:

> *"To understand advertising correctly or to learn even its rudiments you have to start with the correct conception. Advertising is an art of selling. Its principles are the principles of the art of selling. The successes and failures in both lines are due to similar causes. Therefore, each advertising question must be answered according to the vendor's standards.*

Let's emphasize that point. The only purpose of advertising is to make sales. It's profitable or not according to your actual sales.

It's not a general effect. It's not to keep your name in front of the people. It's not primarily to help your other salespeople. Treat him like a salesman. Forcing him to justify himself. Compare it with other vendors. Calculate your cost and result.

Don't accept excuses that good sellers don't make. Then you won't be much wrong.

The difference is only in the degree. Advertising is a multiplication of sales capacity. It can attract thousands while the salesman talks to one. It involves a corresponding cost. Some people spend $10 per word on an average ad. Therefore, each ad must be a super-seller.

A salesman's mistake can cost little. An advertiser's mistake can cost a thousand times more. Be more cautious, more demanding, therefore. A mediocre salesperson can affect a small part of your business. Mediocre advertising affects all your businesses. "

These points are as true today as they were when they were written almost a hundred years ago!

So the goal is: **how can we make our advertising as effective as possible?**

The answer is to try. Try again. And then try some more.

If ad A receives a two percent response rate, and ad B receives three percent, then we can deduce that ad B will continue to outperform ad A on a larger scale.

However, testing takes time and can be costly if not kept under control. Therefore, it is ideal to start with some known and tested ideas and work from there.

For example, if tests have shown for decades or more that targeted advertising significantly outperforms untargeted advertising (and it does!), then we can start with that assumption and continue from there.

If we know, based on the results of the tests, that creating an advertisement that speaks directly to an individual is better than addressing the masses (again, it does), then it makes little sense to start testing with the assumption that it does not. This is common sense.

Therefore, it is logical that knowing some basic rules or techniques for writing an effective copy is the right thing to do. Test results will always triumph over everything, but it is better to have a starting point before the test.

So this starting point is the essence of this book.

The ten tips expressed here have generally been tested over time and are known to be effective.

But I cannot emphasize enough that when using these techniques, they should always be tested before launching a large (and expensive) campaign.

Sometimes a small adjustment here or there is all that is needed to increase response rates drastically.

And with that, let's move on.....

TIP 1: FOCUS ON THEM, NOT ON YOURSELF

When a prospect reads your ad, letter, brochure, etc., the only thing you'll ask from the beginning is, "What's in it for me?"

And if your copy doesn't tell you, it will fall into the trash faster than he can read the headline.

Many advertisers make this mistake. They focus on them as a company. How long they've been in business, who their biggest customers are, how they've spent ten years of research and millions of dollars developing this product, blah, blah, blah...

Actually, those points are important. Remember, once you've thrown it away, the sale is lost!

When you write your copy, it is helpful to think of it as writing a letter to an old friend. In fact, I often imagine a friend of mine who best fits my prospect's profile. What would I say to convince this friend to try my product? How would I address my friend's objections and beliefs to help *my cause?*

When you write to a friend, you'll use the pronouns me and you. When you try to convince your friend, you might say, "Look, I know you think you've tried every product out there. But you should know that....."

And it goes beyond writing in the second person. I mean, address his prospect like <u>you</u> inside the copy. The fact is that there are many successful ads that *were not* written in the second person. Some are written in first-person perspective, where the writer uses <u>me</u>. Other times the third person is used, with <u>her</u>, <u>him</u>, and <u>them</u>.

And even *if* you write in the second person, it doesn't necessarily mean that your copy is about them.

For example:

- As a real estate agent, you can be sure that I have sold more than 10,000 homes and have mastered selling techniques.

Even if you write in the second person, you still focus on yourself.

Then how *can you* concentrate on them? I'm glad you asked. One way is....

TIP 2: EMPHASIZE BENEFITS, NOT FEATURES

What are characteristics? These are descriptions of the qualities a product possesses.

- The XYZ car offers 55 miles per gallon in the city.
- The frame of our staircase is made of a lightweight and durable steel alloy.
- Our tail is protected by a patent.
- This database has a built-in data mining system.

And what are the benefits? They are what those characteristics mean to their prospects.

- You'll save money on gasoline *and reduce* environmental pollutants when you use our high-performance, energy-saving hybrid car. Plus, you'll feel the extra *boost* when you pass in front of the cars, thanks to the efficient electric motor, which *they don't have!*
- The lightweight, durable alloy steel frame means you can take it easily and use it where most other ladders can't go, while supporting up to 800 pounds. No more backaches dragging that heavy ladder. And it will last 150 years, so you'll never have to buy another ladder again!
- Patent-protected glue guarantees its use on wood, plastic, metal, ceramics, glass and tiles... without the

need to clean and without having to re-glue it...
Guaranteed!

- You can instantly see the big picture hidden in your data, and get the most complex statistics on demand. Watch your business make a 180-degree turn in the blink of an eye, when you instantly know why you're failing in the first place! It's all done with our integrated data mining system that is so easy to use that my twelve year old son used it successfully from the *very first moment.*

I just made up those examples, but I think you understand me.

That's why: you don't write to impress your professor of grmática or to win any prize. The only prize you're looking for is that your copy overcomes control (control being the best-selling copy so far), so take some freedom in grammar, punctuation and sentence structure. You want people to read and act accordingly, not read and admire!

But getting back to the benefits....

If you were selling an expensive watch, wouldn't you tell your reader that the dial has a diameter of 2 inches and the strap is made of leather?

Show him how the extra-large face will tell him time at a glance. No, sir! You won't have to squint and look silly to everyone around you trying to read this magnificent watch. And what about the way you will project success and charisma when you wear the beautiful gold watch with your handmade leather strap? How your lover will find you irresistible when dressed to go out, wearing the watch. Or how the state and beauty of the watch will attract the ladies.

By the way, have you noticed that I brought up the issue of *not squinting* as a benefit? Does that sound like a silly benefit? Not if you're selling to wealthy baby boomers who suffer from degrading vision. They probably hate it when someone they're trying to impress sees them squinting to read something. It's all part of his inner desire, which you have to discover. And _they_ don't even know. That is, until you show them a better way.

The point is to address the benefits of the product, not its characteristics. And when you do that, you concentrate on your reader and his interests, his desires. The trick is to highlight the specific benefits (and express them correctly) that push your reader's emotional buttons.

How do you do that? Keep reading!

TIP 3: PRESS YOUR EMOTIONAL BUTTONS

This is where the research really pays off. Because to press those buttons, first you have to know what they are.

Listen to this story first, and I'll tell you what I mean: Once upon a time there was a young man who entered the showroom of a Chevrolet dealer to see a Chevy Camaro. He had the money and was ready to make a buying decision. But he couldn't decide if he wanted to buy the Camaro or the Ford Mustang at the Ford dealership.

A salesman approached him and soon discovered the man's dilemma. "Tell me what you like most about the Camaro," said the salesman. "-It's a _fast_ car. I like it for its speed."

After a little more discussion, the salesman found out that the man had just started dating a pretty college cheerleader. And what did the salesman do?

Simple. He changed his tone accordingly, to press the buttons he knew would help him advance the sale. He told the man how impressed his new girlfriend would be _when she got home with this car._ He put the mental image in the mind of the man of him and his girlfriend sailing towards the beach on the Camaro. How all his friends will become envious when they see him walking with a beautiful girl in a beautiful car.

And suddenly the man saw it. He's done it. And the salesman recognized this and stacked it even more. Before you know it, the man wrote a fat check to the Chevy dealership, because *they sold* it!

The salesman found those buttons and pressed them like never before until the man realized he wanted the Camaro more than he wanted his money.

I know what you're thinking...... The man said he liked the car because it was fast, right?

Yes, he did. But unconsciously, what he really wanted was a car that would impress his girlfriend, his friends, and in his mind make them love him more. In his mind he equated speed with emotion. Not because I wanted an endless supply of speeding fines, but because I thought that emotion would make it more attractive, more enjoyable.

Maybe the man didn't even realize it. But the salesman did. And I knew which emotional buttons to press to get the sale.

Now, to what do we owe the investigation?

Well, a good salesman knows how to ask the kind of questions that will tell him which buttons to press on the fly. When you write texts, you don't have that luxury. Therefore, it is very important to know beforehand the desires, needs and desires of your prospects for that very reason. If you haven't done your homework, your prospect will decide that he would rather keep your money than buy your product. Remember, copywriting is a **print sale!**

It has been said many times: <u>People don't like to be sold.</u>

But they like to shop.

And they buy on the basis of emotion in the first place. Then they justify their decision logically, *even after they have been sold emotionally*. So be sure to back up your emotional tone with logic to nurture that justification in the end.

And while we're at it, let's talk for a moment about what we perceive in a sales letter. Many more conservative advertisers have decided that they don't like the hype, because they consider the hype to be old news, that it's been there but that their customers won't fall for the hype, that it's no longer credible.

What they should realize is that advertising itself does not sell well. Less experienced editors often try to compensate for their lack of research or do not fully understand their target market or the product itself by adding tons of adjectives and adverbs and exclamation marks and large bold letters.

But if you do your job well, you don't have to.

That doesn't mean that some adverbs or adjectives don't have their place... only if they are used in moderation, and only if *they advance in the sale*.

But I think you would agree that backing up your copy with evidence and credibility will be far more convincing to convince your prospects than powerful words alone. I say *powerful words*, because there are certain adverbs and adjectives that *have* proven to make a difference when included. This in itself is not an exaggeration. But if they are repeated too often, they lose effectiveness and take away (at least in your prospect's mind) the proof.

Which brings us to our next tip.....

TIP 4: INCORPORATING EVIDENCE AND CREDIBILITY

When your prospect reads your ad, you want to make sure he creates any claims you make about your product or service. Because if there's any doubt in his mind, he won't bite, no matter how sweet the deal. In fact, the mentality of *too good to be true* will virtually guarantee a lost sale... even if it's all true.

So what can you do to increase the *perception* of credibility? Because after all, it's the perception you have to address from the beginning. But, of course, you must also make sure that your copy is accurate and truthful.

Here are some tried and tested methods that will help you:

- If you're dealing with existing customers who already know you're delivering, emphasize that trust. Don't let them find out. Make them stop, cock their heads and say: -Oh, yes. ABC has never hurt me before. I can trust them.
- Include testimonials from satisfied customers. Be sure to put full names and locations, when possible. Remember, -A.S. is much less credible than Andy Sherman, Voorhees, NJ. If you can also include a photo of the client and a professional title, that's even better. It doesn't matter that your testimonials aren't from someone famous or that your prospect doesn't know these people personally. If you have enough

compelling testimonials, and they are credible, you are much better off not including them at all.

- Season your copy with research facts and findings to support your claims. Be sure to give credit to all sources, even if the fact is in the public domain, as a neutral source contributes greatly to credibility.
- In the case of a direct mail letter or certain space advertisements where the copy is in the form of a letter from a specific person, it helps to include a photo of that person. But unlike traditional real estate letters and other similar advertisements, I would put the photo at the end near your signature, or halfway through the copy, rather than at the top where it would detract from its holder's value. And, if your sales letter *is* from a specific individual, be sure to include your credentials to establish you as an expert in your field (related to your product or service, of course).
- If applicable, cite any third-party awards or reviews that the product or service has received.
- If you've sold a lot of products, tell him. It's the old owner of 10 million people can't be wrong (they can be, but your prospect will probably take your side in the matter).
- Include a BIG returns policy and _stand firm!_ This is a good business policy. Many times, offering a double money-back guarantee for certain products will result in higher profits. Yes, you will give out more rebates, but if you sell three times as many products as before, and you only have to give back twice as

much as before, it may be worth it, depending on your offer and the return on investment. Cross the numbers and see what makes sense. More importantly, *try!* Make them think, they wouldn't be so generous with returns if they weren't behind their product!

- If you can do that, adding a celebrity endorsement will always help establish credibility. Hey, if Abe Lincoln recommended your product and endorses your claims, it must be true. Here's the idea.
- When it makes sense, use third party testimonials. What are third party testimonials? Here are some examples of a copy of a website I wrote when there were still not many customer testimonials available:

"Spyware has undoubtedly increased exponentially over the past six months."

[Alfred Huger, Senior Director of Engineering, Symantec Security Response (manufacturer of Norton security software)]

"Simply by clicking on a banner ad you can install spyware."

[Dave Methvin, Director of Technology, PC Pitstop]

One method of implementation is to "trick users into consenting to a download of software they think they absolutely need.

[Paul Bryan, Director, Security and Technology Unit, Microsoft]

You see what I did?

I took appointments from experts in their respective fields and put them on my side. But be sure to get your consent or permission from the copyright holder if you have any questions about copyrighted materials as your source.

Note that I also pressed an emotional button: fear.

It has been proven that people generally do more to avoid pain than to get pleasure. So why not use that information to your advantage?

Reveal a defect on your product. This helps alleviate the syndrome too good to be true. You reveal a defect that's not really a defect. Or you reveal a defect that is minor, only to show that you are being honest about your product's deficiencies.

Example

> *"You're probably thinking right now that this tennis racket works miracles and it does. But I gotta tell you, he's got a little... defect.*
>
> *My racket takes about two weeks to get used to. In fact, when you start using it for the first time, your game <u>will get worse</u>. But if you can hold on, you'll see a tremendous improvement in your volleys, in the net game, in the serves, ...".* And so on.

There is a tendency to think, with all the ads that bombard us today, that each advertiser is always putting his best foot forward, so to speak. And I think that line of reasoning is correct, to some extent.

But isn't it refreshing when someone stands out from the crowd and is honest? In other words, your reader will begin to subconsciously believe that you are revealing all the faults, even if your best foot is *still* standing.

Use annotations. This is a brief note or letter from a person in authority. You don't need a celebrity, although that can also add credibility. A person with authority is someone well recognized in their field (which is related to their product) and is qualified to talk about it. Elevation notes can be distributed as supplements, on a separate page, or even as part of the copy.

If you are limiting the offer with a deadline, make sure the deadline is real and does not change. Deadlines that change every day are sure to reduce credibility. The prospectus will be suspicious. If your deadline keeps changing, you're not telling the truth about it... I wonder what else isn't telling the truth.

Avoid the unfounded. I talked about that in my previous council.

Enough said.

TIP 5: THE UNIQUE SALE PROPOSAL (USP)

Also known as the unique selling *position*, the *Unique Selling Proposition (*USP) is often one of the most misunderstood elements of a good sales letter. It's what separates your product or service from your competitors. Let's take a look at some unique sales proposals for a product itself:

1. **Lower price** - If you have a discounted price promotion, brag about it. Wal-Mart has made this USP famous lately, but it's not something new to them. In fact, the cheapest sale has existed as long as capitalism itself. Personally, I don't like price wars, because there is always someone who can come and sell cheaper. So it's time for a new strategy....

2. **Superior Quality** - If you outperform your competition's product or are made with higher quality materials, it is a good bet that you can use this fact to your advantage. For example, compare Breyers Ice Cream to your competitor's ice cream. From packaging to healthy, superior ingredients, quality is evident. It may cost a little more than your competitor's ice cream, but for your market, it sells.

3. **Superior Service** - If you offer superior service to your competition, people will buy from you. This is particularly true for certain markets in the service sector: telephony, Internet service providers, cable television, etc.

4. **Exclusive rights** - My favourite! If you can legitimately claim that your product is protected by a patent or copyright, a license agreement, etc., then you have a winner for the exclusive rights. If you have a patent, even the *President of the United States* must buy it from you.

Okay, what if your product or service is no different than your competitor's? I don't agree, because there are always differences. The trick is to turn them into a positive advantage for you. You want to put your best foot forward. What can we do on this stage?

One way is to present something that your company has devised internally and that no other company does. Look, there's a reason why computer store A offers to outbid its competitor's price for the same product by X%. If you look closely, the two packages are never exactly the same. Company B offers a free scanner, while Company A offers a free printer. Or some other difference. They're comparing apples to oranges. So unless you find a company with exactly the same package (you don't.... they've taken care of that), you won't be able to collect.

But what if you really have the same product for sale as the competition?

Unless your prospect knows the inner workings of your product and your competition, including the manufacturing process, customer service and everything else, then you have a small potential creative license here.

But you have to be honest.

For example, if I tell my readers that my product is steam-coated to ensure purity and cleanliness (like cans and bottles in most brewing processes), it doesn't matter that Joe's Beer does the same. Joe's failure to announce this fact makes him a USP in the eyes of his prospect.

Want more examples of USP?

- We're the only auto repair shop that *will buy your car* if you're not 100 percent satisfied with our work.
- Delivered in 30 minutes or we won't charge you!
- No other furniture company will be responsible for shipping costs.
- Our recipe is so secret that only three people in the world know it!

As with most ways to increase copy response, research is the key with your USP. Sometimes your USP is obvious, for example, if you have a patent. Other times you have to do some preliminary work to find out (or adapt it to your target market).

This is where a little persistence and in-person selling really pays off.

Let me give you an example to illustrate what I mean:

Suppose your company sells pouf chairs for children. So you, being the wise salesperson you are, decide to sell these chairs in person to potential customers before writing your copy. After completing twenty different launches for your product, you discover that 75 percent of those you visited asked if the chair would eventually leak. Since the chairs are for children, it's logical that parents worry about their child jumping on them, rolling on them, and doing everything possible to break the seam.

Therefore, when writing your text, be sure to address this problem: -You can be sure that our super-strong pouf chairs are sewn into three points to ensure leak-proof performance. No other company will make this warranty on your pouf chairs!

TIP 6: THE HOLDER

If you're going to make just one change to increase your response rate to the maximum, focus on your holder (you have one, don't you?).

Why is that? I don't know. Because there are <u>five times more</u> people reading your headline than your entire ad. Simply put, a headline is... an ad for your ad. People won't stop in their busy lives to read your ad unless you give them a good reason to do so. So a good headline promises some news and a benefit.

Maybe you're thinking, "What's this news thing, you say?

Think about the last time you looked at your local newspaper. You reviewed the articles, one by one, and occasionally an ad may have caught your attention. Which ads caught your attention the most?

The ones that looked like an article, of course.

The ones with the headline that promised news.

Those who had fonts and types that closely resembled the fonts and types used in the articles.

Those that were placed where the items were placed (as opposed to those that were placed on a full page of ads, for example).

And those who have the most compelling headlines that convinced you that it's worth reading the copy.

The headline is _that_ powerful and _that_ important.

I've seen a lot of ads over the years that didn't even _have_ a headline. And that's nonsense. It's the equivalent of flushing advertising money down the toilet.

Why is that? I don't know. Because your response can dramatically increase not only by adding a headline, but by making that headline almost impossible to resist _for your target market_.

And those last three words are important. **Your target market.**

For example, take a look at the following headline:

AD: The new high-tech gloves protect the user against hazardous waste.

News, and a benefit.

Will it be a headline that will attract everyone?

No, and you don't care about everyone.

But for someone who handles hazardous waste, I'm sure he'd appreciate to know about this little jewel.

That's your target market, and it's your job to make them read your ad. Your headline is the way you do it.

Okay, where do you find the big headlines?

You look at other successful ads (especially direct response) that have stood the test of time. You are looking for ads that are regularly published in magazines and other publications.

How do you know they are good? Because if they didn't do their job, the advertiser wouldn't keep running them over and over again.

You enter the mailing lists of large direct response companies such as Agora and Boardroom and save your direct mail packages.

You read the National Enquirer.

Huh? [Laughs] You heard right.

The National Enquirer has some of the best headlines in the business.

Pick a recent number and you'll see what I mean. Okay, now, how could you adapt some of those headlines to your own product or service?

Your headline should create a sense of urgency. It should be as specific as possible (e.g. $1,007,274.23 instead of $1 million).

The appearance of the headlines is also very important. Make sure the type used is bold and large, and different from the type used in the copy. Generally, longer headlines tend to be shorter, even when aimed at a more conservative audience.

Needless to say, when you use other successful headlines, you adapt them to your own product or service. Never copy a headline (or any other copyrighted work) word for word. Copywriters and advertising agencies are famous for suing for plagiarism. And rightly so.

TIP 7: THE MORE BEADS, THE MORE YOU SELL

The debate on the use of long copies versus short copies seems never to end. He is usually a newcomer to copywriting who seems to think long text is boring and, well.... long. -I'd never read so many copies, they say.

The fact is, if all things are the same, long copies always outnumber short ones. And when I say a long copy, I don't mean long and boring, or long and aimless.

The person who says he would never read all that text is making a big mistake in writing: he is being carried away by his visceral reaction instead of relying on the test results. He's thinking he's the prospect himself. No, it's not. We're never our own prospects.

Many studies and divisional evidence have been conducted in the debate of long versus short copying. And the clear winner is always a long copy. But that's a long, relevant, directed copy, rather than a long, boring, undirected copy.

Some significant research has found that readership tends to fall dramatically by about 300 words, but does not fall back by as much as 3,000 words.

If I am selling an expensive set of golf clubs and sending my long copy to a person who plays golf occasionally, or who has always wanted to try golf, I am sending my sales pitch to the wrong prospect. It's not an effective target. And if a person who receives my long copy does not read beyond the word number 300, he was not qualified for my offer in the first place.

It wouldn't have mattered if they'd read up to the word 100 or the word 10,000. They still wouldn't have made a purchase.

However, if I sent my long copy to an avid golfer, who recently bought other expensive golf products by mail, painting him an irresistible offer, telling him how my clubs will take 10 strokes off his game, he'll probably read every word. And if I've addressed my message correctly, he'll buy it.

Remember, if your prospect is 3000 miles away, it's not easy for him to ask you a question. You must anticipate and answer all your questions and overcome all objections in your copy if you want to succeed.

And make sure you don't throw everything you can think of in the sun. You just need to include as much information as you need to make the sale... and not a word more.

If you need a 10-page sales letter, so be it. If you need a 16-page catalog, fine. But if the 10-page sales letter is better than the 16-page catalog, then, of course, go with the winner.

Does that mean that every prospect must read every word of your copy before ordering your product? Of course you don't.

Some will read every word and then read it again. Some will read the headline and headline, and then read much of the body and go all the way. Some will explore the whole body and then read it again. All these prospects may end up buying the offer, but they may also have different reading styles.

Which brings us to the next tip.....

TIP 8: WRITING TO BE SCANNED

Your design is very important in a sales letter, because you want your letter to look attractive and refreshing to the eyes. In short, you want your prospect to stop doing what he or she is doing and read your letter.

If you see a letter with tiny margins, no indentations, no breaks in the text, no blank spaces, no subtitles... if you see a page with only densely filled words, do you think he will be tempted to read it?

Not likely.

If you have ample white space and generous margins, short sentences, short paragraphs, subtitles, and an italicized or underlined word here and there to emphasize, you'll certainly be more attractive to read.

As you read your letter, some prospects will start at the beginning and read word for word. Some will read the headline and perhaps the headline, then read the postscript at the end of the letter and see whose letter it is, and then start from the beginning.

And some people will review your letter, noting the various subheadings strategically placed by you throughout your letter, and then decide whether it is worth reading the letter in its entirety. Some may never read the whole letter, but order anyway.

You must write for all of them. Interesting and compelling long text for the studious reader, and short paragraphs and sentences, white space and subtitles.

Subtitles are the smallest headlines splashed all over your copy.

Just like that.

When you come up with a headline, some of the headlines that didn't make it to court can be big subheadings. A good subtitle forces your prospectus to keep reading, threading it from start to finish through its entire copy, while also providing you with the glue needed to keep prospects reading.

TIP 9: THE STRUCTURE OF AIDAS

There is a well known structure to successful sales letters, described by the acronym *AIDA*.

AIDA means:

- Attention
- Interest
- Desire
- Action

First, you get your prospect's attention. This is done with the headline and the header. If your ad does not capture the attention of your prospect, it fails completely. Your prospectus does not read your star copy, and does not order your product or service.

So you want to build a strong interest in your prospect. You want me to keep reading, because if I read, I could buy.

Then you channel a wish. Having a target market for this is key, because it's not about creating a desire where it didn't already exist. You want to capitalize on an existing wish, which your prospect *may or may not know you already have.* And you want your prospect to experience that desire for your product or service.

Finally, you present a call to action. You want me to pick up the phone, return the reply card, attend the sales presentation, order your product, whatever. You need to ask for the sale (or answer, if that is the goal). You don't want to beat around the bush at this point. If your charter and AIDA's structure are solid and persuasive, this is where you present the terms of your offer and urge the prospect to act now.

Much has been written about AIDA's drafting formula. I would like to add one more letter to the acronym: S for Satisfaction.

In the end, after the sale, you want to satisfy your potential customer, who is now a customer. You want to deliver exactly what you promised (or even more), on the date you promised, in the following way that you promised. In short, you want to give him all the reasons in the world to trust you the next time he sells you an offer. And of course you would prefer that I don't return the product (although if I do, you also execute your return policy *as promised*).

Either way, you want your customers to be satisfied. It'll make you a lot more money in the long run.

TIP 10: USE YOUR AD TO INCREASE URGENCY

When the supply of a product or service is limited in some way (e.g., limited sales), the basic economy dictates that demand will increase. In other words, people will generally respond better to an offer if they believe the offer is about to become unavailable or restricted in some way.

And of course, the opposite is also true. If a prospect knows that his product will be available when he needs it, he doesn't need to act now. And when the prospect leaves his ad aside, the possibility of closing the sale decreases enormously.

It is your job, therefore, to get your prospect to buy, and to buy now.

Using scarcity to sell is a great way to do it.

There are basically three types of product limitations:

1. Quantity limitation
2. Limitation in time
3. Limitation of the offer

In the first method, by limiting the quantity, a fixed number of products are presented available for sale. After they've run out, that's all.

Some good ways to limit the amount include:

- a limited number of units manufactured or obtained

- sell old products to make room for new ones
- limited number of aesthetically faulty items, or a flash sale
- only a limited number is sold so as not to saturate the market

In the second method, which limits time, a time limit is added to the offer. It should be a realistic deadline, not one that changes all the time (especially on a website, where the deadline always seems to be the same day at midnight...). when you return the next day, the deadline has mysteriously changed back to the new day). Changing deadlines diminish your credibility.

This approach works well when the offer or price changes, or when the product/service ceases to be available after the deadline.

The third method, which limits the offer, is done by limiting other parts of the offer, such as the guarantee, the bonds or premiums, the price, etc.

When you use the limited sale, you must make sure you comply with its restrictions. If you say you only have 500 products to sell, then don't sell 501. If you say your offer will expire at the end of the month, make sure it does. Otherwise, your credibility will be affected. Prospects will remember the next time another offer of theirs comes into their hands.

Another important thing you should do is explain why the offer is being restricted. Don't just say the price will go up in three weeks, but don't tell them why.

Here are some examples of good sales to go:

- Unfortunately, I can't handle that many customers. Once my quota is full, I won't be able to accept any new business. So if you really want to strengthen your investment strategies and create more wealth than ever, you should contact me as soon as possible.
- Remember.... you must act by [date] midnight in order to receive my 2 bonuses. These bonuses have been provided by [third company], and we have no control over their availability after that time.
- We have obtained only 750 of these premiums from our supplier. Once they're gone, we can't get any more until next year. And yet we cannot guarantee that the price will remain the same. In fact, due to growing demand, the price is likely to double or triple by then!

Remember when I said before that people buy on the basis of emotions and then support their decision to buy logically? Well, by using take-away selling, that restriction becomes part of that buy-and-buy logic now.

Conclusion

You do a great copywriting, you're not born. It is derived from proven test results designed to do one thing and do it well: sell.

Effective advertising does not always use "grammatically correct" text. Use short phrases, fragments. Just like that.

It convinces you to buy, and buy now. That's it.

He's talking about benefits, not features. He sells for excitement and reinforces the decision to buy logically.

It paints a compelling picture and an irresistible offer that forces your prospect to act and act now! And if it doesn't, then you drop that ad like a hot potato and go with one that does.

Effective persuasion is like your best salesman, the one who keeps beating all your sales records year after year, working 24 hours a day, 7 days a week, multiplied by thousands or millions. Imagine if that the seller, the one who has proven results, could multiply as much as you would like.

That would be effective (and profitable) marketing!

And that's the kind of proven marketing you need to employ.

About the Author

Faustino Gómez Valero is a Technical Engineer in Computer Management and Master in Creation of Technological Companies by the University of Murcia.

His work experience of almost 20 years is closely linked to the world of technology and finance. He complements his studies with the title of Financial Advisor and the Specialization in Big Data by the University of California, San Diego.

He published his first book in 2001 and, although he has not published any more until 2019, he has trained with the best international experts in the sectors of financial investment, digital marketing and entrepreneurship.

He lives in a quiet town in the province of Alicante (Spain) with his family.

Faustino is a Digital Nomad and Entrepreneur, he loves to educate and inspire other authors and entrepreneurs to succeed.

You can find out more or contact Faustino through Linkedin: https://www.linkedin.com/in/faustinogomez/

ONE LAST THING...

If you liked this book, or found it useful, we would be very grateful if you would publish a review on Amazon.

Your support helps us a lot, and your criticism helps us to constantly improve in order to provide better content.

Thank you for your support!